I, You
Could
Ask
God

To Jill —
Thanks for your help
with the back cover copy!

Wishing you many blessings,

Jeff Keller

If You Could Ask God

347 questions that only God could answer on faith, love, good and evil, nature and more . . .

Compiled by Jeff Keller and John Lisicich

Attitude is Everything, Inc.
East Norwich, NY

LCCN: 2006909073

ISBN 13: 978-0-9790410-0-6
ISBN 10: 0-9790410-0-7

Printed in the United States of America

Introduction

If you could ask God three questions, what would you ask?

Would you ask about life after death? Or good and evil? Would you want to know about the secrets of nature or the universe? Or perhaps you would just like to know what God is, after all. There are a million questions that are so personal, so difficult, or so impossible to answer, that we can only pose them to God.

For three years, we invited people of all ages, religions, and nationalities to submit their questions to God, in person and over the internet. Thus far, we've received over 6,000 fascinating, challenging, entertaining, and thought-provoking questions, and we've picked 347 of them to include in this book.

You won't find any answers in this book, but you will find questions that make you think, laugh, and learn. You'll learn about other people, and you'll learn a lot about yourself. We encourage you to discuss these questions with others, because we guarantee that a stimulating discussion will ensue.

We hope you enjoy the book and we wish you many blessings on your journey.

— Jeff Keller and John Lisicich

1

Do you find all this praising of you
annoying?

— Ed, age 43

2

How do you feel about all these
television ministries?

— John, age 50

3

Where does this seemingly inherent
need for "more" come from?

— Mark, age 40

4

How close is the Bible to fact?

— Rhonda, age 43

5

If you have the ability to make the world a paradise, why do you allow suffering?

— Robert, age 60

6

What is the most enjoyable part of being God?

— Linda, age 31

7

What are ghosts?

— Amy, age 40

8

Is there chocolate in heaven?

— Bev, age 42

9

When I pass on, will there be opportunities to grow spiritually, mentally or in whatever form we are?

— Paul, age 51

10

Do you watch when we make love,
go to the bathroom, or do something
totally embarrassing when we think
no one is watching?

— Pegine, age 45

11

When do I start reading the book I
bought on Procrastination?

— Navia, age 32

12

If you know everything that will
happen, do we really have free will?

— Pamela, age 34

13

Since Adam was not born through a
womb, did he have a belly button?

— Carla, age 33

14

Why don't you make your presence
obvious, undeniable, and crystal clear?

— Wayne, age 37

15

Have you ever thought about
rescinding the gift of free will you have
given us?

— Judy, age 39

16

....

Do you ever send good people to hell?

— Roger, age 55

17

....

How are terrorists dealt with in the afterlife?

— John, age 66

18

....

Don't you think it's time to send a powerful messenger — one that speaks a common language?

— James, age 57

19
....

Are there sports or competitive opportunities in heaven?

— Richard, age 50

20

Why does it take a crisis to bring
people together to pray?

— Deborah, age 51

21

When you created the mosquito, what
were you thinking?

— Kim, age 48

22

After death, will we be reunited with
friends and family who have also died?

— Teresa, age 52

23

How can I attract what I want into my
life?

— *Stan, age 55*

24

How does a thermos know the
difference between hot and cold?

— *James, age 38*

25

Why do those who have faith in you
not have faith in themselves?

— *Elizabeth, age 40*

26

If a human embryo is cloned, does it have a soul and is it the same soul each time it is cloned?

— Ellen, age 21

27

What is your definition of love?

— Carol, age 49

28

If people go to hell, is there a way to get back to heaven?

— Heidi, age 32

29

Why is your plan and purpose for my
life such a mystery?

— Alice, age 41

30

Would you please explain how the
seven wonders of the world came into
existence?

— Betty, age 38

31

How can we get people to look for the
positives in any negative situation?

— Amanda, age 55

32

Are there other beings in the universe
with a soul, or are we it?

— Patricia, age 42

33

Why don't we remember where we
were before we were born?

— Wanda, age 33

34

What do you think about cloning?

— Caroline, age 60

35

Are you directly or indirectly involved
in day-to-day events?

— Andrew, age 65

36

Why is yawning contagious?

— Sarah, age 43

37

Why do you allow so much confusion
as to which is the right religion, to the
point where millions of people have
been killed in your name over the
centuries?

— Justin, age 47

38

Why did you make poison ivy?

— Eileen, age 9

39

Where did you get all the different ideas for your creations?

— Sandra, age 60

40

Does everyone in heaven get to meet you personally?

— Brent, age 40

41

What is more important — the faith we choose to worship you, or the actual actions to follow your word as best as we can?

— John, age 40

42

My favorite sound is when a baby laughs. What is your favorite sound?

— Gina, age 45

43

Are you really there?

— Bonnie, age 23

44

Will all my questions about this life be answered in the next?

— Ron, age 48

45

Who or what is Satan, and how much power does he possess?

— Carl, age 31

46

Have you ever thought about throwing in the towel?

— Candace, age 54

47

What are the ingredients for success?

— Bill, age 40

48

Is it okay for one's aim in life to be
earning lots of money?

— Ron, age 40

49

What is your definition of a hero?

— Doris, age 58

50

What do you think about all the
religions using guilt to keep their
members in check?

— Sally, age 28

51

Do I have a heart like yours?

— Julie, age 35

52

Which of all the religions in the world
is the closest to the truth?

— Joaquin, age 40

53

If you could go back, would you create
everything the same way or would you
make changes?

— Martinetti, age 29

54

Did all humans descend from Adam and Eve?

— Denise, age 46

55

Do bad people like Hitler get theirs in the end?

— Cathi, age 46

56

Do you ever feel pressure because so many people look up to you?

— Melanie, age 11

57

Is there really a Hell?

— Theresa, age 36

58

What are the things you expect from us?

— Midnighter, age 18

59

Why can't everybody be beautiful?

— Beth, age 14

60

Can you take a joke?

— Janice, age 44

61

Is Heaven large enough to hold everyone?

— Diane, age 54

62

Who really built the pyramids and how?

— Danette, age 38

63

Can you explain infinity?

— Anne, age 41

64

Since the beginning of time, what
would you say is the most miraculous
thing that has happened in the world?

— Jo, age 55

65

Why are women so much more
understanding than men?

— Dean, age 39

66

If it's so much better in Heaven, why
are we "required" to live our lives here?

— Linda, age 42

67

How do you choose who to answer when two people are praying something exactly opposite of each other?

— Donna, age 51

68

Why did you create fleas?

— Polly, age 65

69

When judgment day arrives, will you be factoring in the culture of our times?

— Irene, age 32

70

Why do you want us to worship you?

— Ratu, age 35

71

When I've tried everything and prayed
and prayed and prayed and my prayers
still aren't answered, what do I do?

— Omeria, age 45

72

Why cause so much weather-related
destruction in the world?

— Aida, age 43

73

Why is the aging process necessary in our journey here on Earth?

— Richard, age 63

74

Do you consider all sins to be of equal seriousness?

— Bud, age 47

75

Does our choice of religion really affect whether we are granted your forgiveness and everlasting life?

— Sunshine, age 28

76

Can you show me the lives I have touched (positively), both directly and indirectly?

— Amy, age 30

77

If you could change two things about me, what would they be?

— Rosie, age 35

78

What goes on up there all day?

— Andrea, age 34

79

Do you see all religions as honoring
you, but just in a different way?

— Christa, age 36

80

What would you say to people who
don't believe in the Bible or you?

— Sarah, age 14

81

Why are we not able to see you?

— Fakhruddin, age 52

82

Why don't you do something to convince the skeptics that there is a God and that you do miracles?

— Narayanan, age 30

83

Will there be a time when the world will be united and free of problems?

— Abhishek, age 28

84

Why do I thank you when good things happen yet do not blame you when bad things happen?

— Linda, age 51

85

Why do we push harder on the buttons of the remote control when we know the batteries are dead?

— Amber, age 19

86

Do those who live with you now in the afterlife see us, or is there a barrier that separates the two worlds?

— Jim, age 48

87

Do my prayers change your mind, or my attitude?

— Jeff, age 25

88

Do we all have guardian angels, and how do we contact them?

— Alan, age 39

89

When did the dinosaurs roam the
earth and why aren't they mentioned
in the Bible?

— Nancy, age 50

90

Do animals have souls?

— Lisa, age 30

91

Why did you have women evolve past
the Neanderthal stage but not men?

— Melody, age 46

92

Why do you let bad things happen to good people?

— Diane, age 65

93

Why does every existing religion believe that **theirs** is the only true interpretation of the existence, purpose, and meaning of life?

— Patsy, age 45

94

Are there any other people in the universe on planets like earth?

— Craig, age 38

95

Having never been exposed to religion during my youth, how would I know which to believe as truth?

— Dawn, age 41

96

How does one little sperm and one little egg turn out to be me?

— Yvonne, age 59

97

Do you decide who falls in love with who?

— Beth, age 14

98

What is the purpose of sex from a
spiritual standpoint?

— David, age 54

99

What do I have to trade in to win a
mega lotto?

— Anthony, age 35

100

What do you think about those fish
decals on the backs of cars?

— Tricia, age 33

101

When you put obstacles in my way,
how do I know whether you are testing
me, or trying to tell me this is not
what you prepared for me?

— Andrej, age 35

102

Could I watch while you create a
human being?

— Jan, age 44

103

If you are all knowing, why go through
the exercise of creating a world just to
watch it self-destruct?

— Leann, age 43

104

Would you mind telling me when I'm going to die?

— Arthur, age 27

105

If you are a God of love and compassion how can you stand to see the horrors in the world, and why don't you step in?

— John, age 44

106

What is most important?

— Joseph, age 47

107
....

Have you ever thought a degree of regulation of man's total free will may have been a good idea?

— Jim, *age* 41

108

What do you look like?

— Bryce, age 4

109

If forgiveness is so important, why
didn't you just forgive Adam and Eve?

— Sharina, age 38

110

Which did come first — the chicken or
the egg?

— Mitch, age 40

111

Do you laugh more at me or with me?

— Cyndi, age 40

112

Do you wear clothes in heaven?

— Kelly, age 25

113

Would you let me see what the earth looked like on the seventh day from sunrise to sunset?

— Tiffany, age 28

114

What can I do to make a lasting,
positive change in the world?

— Ed, age 62

115

Are politicians really that stupid, or
are they faking it?

— Luis, age 53

116

When I grow up, can I have my pink
house?

— Cheryl, age 8

117

If you created everything in this world,
then why did you create evil?

— Amit, age 26

118

Why didn't you just make more good
things like trees, flowers, and birds
and skip making bad things like
sickness, hatred, and mean people?

— Megan, age 8

119

May I hug you?

— Terra, age 37

120

When you were creating the earth,
how did you decide to paint the sky
blue and the trees green and so on?

— Karen, age 45

121

How funny is it to watch us interpret
all this stuff?

— Chal, age 45

122

What did you do before you created
the universe?

— Sharon, age 21

123

What would you consider to be good music?

— Josh, age 22

124

What is the most beautiful thing you have ever seen?

— John, age 26

125

What can I do right now to permanently get rid of worrying?

— Annie, age 60

126

....

When I die, how will it feel to move
from the human experience to the
spiritual, and what type of experiences
are waiting for me?

— Michele, age 43

127

....

Can I have your job?

— Chuck, age 43

128

....

Do you forgive divorce?

— Terrie, age 39

129

Why is it that anger and hatred can spread so easily but love and kindness cannot?

— Diana, age 53

130

What thoughts go through my 16-month-old and my 5-month-old babies' minds?

— Melissa, age 22

131

What do you think of organized religion?

— Eileen, age 54

132

What was the point of the Holocaust?

— Michael, age 22

133

Why are we responsible for the sins of Adam and Eve?

— Connie, age 49

134

Why is your plan different from ours?

— Ric, age 25

135

How is my grandpa doing up there?

— Krystal Jo, age 11

136

Why have you made yourself so esoteric that not many people understand you, and they even fight amongst themselves in the name of religion?

— Shankar, age 34

137

Where is Noah's ark?

— Julie, age 31

138

Was Jesus your son?

— Chris, age 39

139

How can I easily know what you created me to come and do in this world?

— Erin, age 44

140

Did you really see me egg those houses when I was twelve?

— Paul, age 25

141

Why do rotten, selfish people live successful lives?

— Joanne, age 43

142

What is my mission in life?

— Carole, age 57

143

What do you want us to call you?

— Robert, age 44

144

Why did you banish us to this universe
of matter, energy, space and time just
to have us claw our way back to where
we came from?

— Vickie, age 47

145

Why did my 3-year-old daughter get leukemia?

— Margie, age 48

146

Where are you?

— Clyde, age 55

147

What can we do differently as individuals to increase love and friendship among the countries of this world?

— Ginger, age 33

148

If you are all good, all forgiving, and all love, how is it possible that we are all created in your image and yet still there is evil?

— Julie, age 42

149

Is there reincarnation, or is that just a fantasy some people believe in to make them feel better?

— Shawn, age 41

150

What is the best way to make money now?

— Iona, age 20

151

Why do many humans believe they are superior to animals?

— Marsha, age 56

152

Why do you allow so many people to live in poverty and squalid conditions, while others live in extreme luxury and comfort?

— Ronald, age 40

153

Do you ever make a mistake?

— Ardeth, age 47

154

Why is there no punishment in the same life span for sinners?

— Ivan, age 35

155

Why did you create this world?

— Punam, age 27

156

Killer bees. Why?

— Meg, age 44

157

Can people who have passed over hear
us if we talk to them?

— Teresa, age 52

158

If you take someone when they are young, does it mean they are so special you needed them early?

— Janine, age 37

159

Why couldn't you just do away with evil from the beginning?

— Lea, age 37

160

How does music work to impact people's soul and emotions so powerfully?

— Jerry, age 41

161

How do you decide who gets born into which family, who gets more brains, who gets more looks, who's gonna die when they're 6 or 106?

— Karly, age 16

162

Why did people in the early days live nine hundred years, while now it has dwindled to eighty or ninety?

— Sheryl, age 56

163

Why didn't you make men the child-bearers?

— Malyssa, age 32

164

In heaven, do we do nothing, or will
we have jobs to keep us busy?

— Billie, age 82

165

Why is it when you live by the Golden
Rule, most other people don't?

— Sheryl, age 57

166

How can I teach a child to believe in
you when her friends have taught her
it's not "cool" to believe in you?

— Pauline, age 40

167

Will you explain to me how women
think?

— Rob, age 18

168

When people are really trying to serve
you and advance your cause, why don't
you give them more help?

— Lola, age 55

169

Is having our own spirituality as
important as structured religion?

— Linda, age 53

170

Why is organized religion so gender based, and how did you let that happen?

— Sue, age 51

171

For what purpose were humans created?

— Laura, age 22

172

If Adam and Eve were the only people on earth, how did their son get married?

— Bev, age 53

173

Do you really know everything about everyone all the time?

— Ron, age 48

174

How did you ever come up with
Spring? I love it!

— Beth, age 54

175

Why isn't everyone healed when prayed
for?

— Helen, age 50

176

How do I know when my thoughts are
all mine, or if you are trying to help
me?

— Brian, age 35

177

If an afterlife exists, why can't you
show more evidence and actual images
of it?

— Donna, age 54

178

What are wasps for?

— Carolyln, age 49

179

Why do you allow innocent children to
be afflicted with such horrific diseases
that make their time on this earth full
of pain and suffering?

— Leigh Anne, age 54

180

Is there really such a thing as soul mates?

— Daree, age 29

181

Did you create the Bible or did mankind create it?

— Jennifer, age 55

182

Why do people question your existence?

— Stacey, age 32

183

What makes you the most angry?

— Tammy, age 45

184

When we pass on, will we look the age at our death or when we were younger?

— Sara, age 68

185

Do we really have free will, or is everything already planned out?

— Tessa, age 19

186

How can you have no beginning and no end?

— Andrew, age 48

187

When you made the world in six days, were they literal 24-hour days?

— Dawn, age 39

188

Why did you put all of the calories in the good stuff?

— Patricia, age 42

189

My daddy died at the World Trade
Tower. Is he with you?

— Emanuel, age 6

190

Why can't we have a glimpse of
paradise to keep us on course?

— Elizabeth, age 42

191

How can we get people to understand
the importance of the ecological
system?

— Fenton, age 35

192

What's the lesson you most want me to learn in this life?

— Marilyn, age 52

193

Are there different levels of heaven so that a person's just reward is appropriate to what they deserve?

— Ron, age 48

194

How do you decide who you are calling home to you first?

— Dean, age 39

195

Why do sweet, likeable babies have to grow into hard-to-understand, bad attitude, lazy teenagers?

— Linda, age 49

196

Why do we have to learn the hard way
all too often?

— Glen, age 24

197

When I think I hear someone speaking
to me, is that your reassuring voice?

— Belinda, age 29

198

How do you answer so many prayers
24/7?

— Betty, age 43

199

If man really descended from Adam
and Eve, why is there so much evidence
of people descending from apes?

— Elizabeth, age 16

200

How do you make people?

— Aubrey, age 5

201

Why is it that the majority of wars are
fought over religion?

— Cindy, age 38

202

What is the Big Plan?

— Carole, age 55

203

When I pass on from this earthly body, will I recognize my mom and my best friend when I get to heaven?

— Nancy, age 50

204

Why all this pain and misery? Why?

— Ethan, age 18

205

Do you outsource?

— Tom, age 49

206

If the human race manages to destroy ourselves, will you start over?

— Lindsey, age 36

207

If love is the greatest gift of all, why does it hurt so bad at times?

— Liz, age 42

208

Do you have a wife up there?

— Moesha, age 6

209

How much and how often should I pray, and what should I pray for specifically?

— Vernon, age 43

210

Can I take a picture of you?

— Kyle, age 5

211

If we do things that are considered
sins, and yet we are forgiven, why
shouldn't we do them and enjoy them
(except for murder)?

— Mary Ann, age 28

212

What are the disadvantages as well as
advantages of being God?

— Linda, age 21

213

What is the secret to happiness?

— Laurie, age 40

214

Why do some people have hardship and suffering while others seem to breeze through life without a care in the world?

— Diana, age 45

215

Do you really love country music?

— Angel, age 42

216

When people pray for a seriously ill person to be healed, why are some healed and others are not?

— Tamara, age 42

217
....

Who on earth is the best source for guidance in following your teachings?

— Sean, age 28

218

If our heart knows what is right, why does our nature say something else?

— Nancy, age 52

219

Why did you create animals and insects that are not useful to the human being?

— Michael, age 30

220

Do soldiers go to heaven?

— Hilary, age 4

221

What's the best way to honor you?

— John, age 55

222

Are you a being or an energy?

— Louise, age 38

223

How much of our lives do we actually
control, and how much is "your plan"
for us?

— Janice, age 41

224

Why do you allow little children to suffer?

— Sharilyn, age 55

225

What is the relationship between you and me?

— Ann, age 50

226

I'm a survivor of the World Trade Center. Why did you spare me?

— Isabel, age 46

227

Why did you let Noah bring roaches on the ark?

— Ingrid, age 38

228

Is the date of our death preordained irrespective of the life choices we make?

— Jenny, age 46

229

Why don't kids come with an instruction manual?

— Rob, age 35

230

Why do you answer certain prayers
and not others?

— Shalina, age 25

231

Can you drive to all the planets?

— Cassidy, age 4

232

How can I see you, talk to you, and feel
you?

— Krishnakum, age 27

233

How can I tell when I am doing my assignment?

— Larry, age 53

234

Can you help the children of the world and keep them from starving?

— Lorraine, age 87

235

Why do centipedes have a hundred legs?

— Willie, age 9

236

Why don't people realize that their happiness lies within them?

— Sandra, age 60

237

Why do anteaters have long noses?

— Kevin, age 9

238

Who made **you**?

— Arthur, age 9

239

How do you pick between two teams praying for a victory?

— Brent, age 40

240

What made you create such a
complicated system called "The
World"?

— Rakesh, age 38

241

Under what circumstances do you
intervene with miracles?

— MJ, age 40

242

Why have you allowed people who
abuse and kill babies and children to
walk the earth?

— John, age 63

243

Why does success come so easily to
some and so hard for others?

— Brice, age 28

244

If all comes from you, where does
injustice, cruelty and betrayal come
from?

— Anil, age 46

245

Do you ever get tired of me asking for
the same things over and over?

— Esther, age 41

246

What should I tell my children when they ask about death?

— Thomas, age 51

247

If you could change one thing in history, what would it be?

— Gerard, age 34

248

What is the solution to global peace?

— Mahesh, age 35

249

Do our loved ones in heaven share our happy times?

— Carol, age 48

250

Who killed JFK and why?

— George, age 57

251

Is the Bermuda Triangle real and if so, what causes it?

— Linda, age 49

252

When is it better to fight than turn the other cheek?

— Chris, age 46

253

When will you manifest yourself?

— Henry, age 57

254

What should I spend my most time doing?

— Scott, age 36

255

What is the definition of the perfect human being?

— Priyanka, age 28

256

Does everything happen for a reason?

— Crystal, age 28

257

How can I attain good health and remain healthy forever?

— Alexander, age 38

258

How can I be more open to your
guidance and instructions?

— William, age 60

259

What is the exact age of this world?

— Oluwole, age 31

260

In heaven, can we do sports, eat
anything, or travel?

— Heidi, age 32

261

Why do I grow hair where I don't want it and lose hair where I want it?

— Shawn, age 34

262

Did we really go to the moon?

— Danette, age 38

263

How can I be sure a decision I make is right for me?

— Kathleen, age 48

264

Why did you put me on this earth?

— Suzanne, age 55

265

What is your e-mail address?

— Sushant, age 30

266

How can I become an instrument of your peace in my little corner of the world?

— Lillian, age 43

267

What happens to us after we die?

— Faiza, age 26

268

What did the oldest man in the Bible
look like before he died?

— Mindy, age 26

269

Why is it so important for you to
remain an unknown?

— Joann, age 34

270

What is the purpose of millions of
sperm being rejected so that only one
can fertilize an egg to create life?

— Steve, age 45

271

Am I even getting close to fulfilling the
purpose you created for me?

— Cyndi, age 40

272

Why are there so many conflicting
religions in the world?

— Diana, age 25

273

What one thing about yourself, that
humans know nothing about, would
you like for us to know at this time?

— Wayne, age 37

274

If you intended us to worship and believe only in you, why did you give us free will?

— Lindsey, age 36

275

Why do some people who are kind and loving leave this earth at a young age, yet the murderers, child molesters and rapists live on?

— Nancy, age 50

276

When I don't receive the things I pray for, is it my lack of faith?

— Joseph, age 47

277

Will the concept of individual earthly families be present in heaven?

— Ron, age 48

278

How big a role do angels play in our lives here on earth?

— Cathy, age 47

279

Who am I?

— Rose, age 42

280

Are there other beings on other planets
whose lives you are also involved in?

— Elizabeth, age 53

281

Why do people have to die?

— Zachary, age 5

282

What can I do for you?

— Amy, age 26

283

How come that when we're just getting the hang of life it's time to die?

— Roy, age 67

284

Why did you have to create snakes?

— Dawn, age 39

285

Why did you invent disease?

— Cindy, age 45

286

Why did you allow polygamy (e.g., King David and King Solomon) among your people in ancient times?

— Pauline, age 48

287

What is the purpose for the other
planets in the solar system?

— Lisa, age 29

288

Can people of all religions get into
heaven?

— Carol, age 37

289

Why are children given more energy
than the parents who are caring for
them?

— Carolyn, age 49

290

Is having sex before marriage a sin?

— Rona, age 18

291

What is it like in the spirit world?

— Mary, age 48

292

Do we choose our own life before we are born?

— Ruth, age 46

293

What are the requirements to get to heaven?

— Ellen, age 21

294

Can I ask an unlimited number of questions?

— Juliana, age 47

295

What's your favorite song?

— Tricia, age 33

296

Do you really prefer the old mushy
opera-style praises and hymns we sing
to you or do you like rap, R&B, pop, or
rock?

— Karly, age 16

297

Why did you take my husband at an
early age when we were married only
five months?

— Marlene, age 45

298

How is it possible that you have always
been?

— Sharon, age 21

299

What is it like to be God?

— Nigel, age 50

300

How do you make rainbows?

— Tiffanie, age 12

301

How long does it take to achieve enlightenment?

— Jeannet, age 39

302

Why didn't you create men with the natural instinct to refill the toilet paper roll when empty?

— Meg, age 44

303

Do you relax?

— Sam, age 48

304

Why was I chosen to have such a hard life?

— Donna, age 50

305

Is life supposed to be complicated and difficult, or am I making a big deal out of something that is supposed to be simple?

— Gina, age 45

306

Is there hope for Satan?

— Bill, age 62

307

How did you come to determine the
five senses we would have as humans?

— Glen, age 24

308

Why don't good people get more
rewards while they're still on earth?

— Diane, age 65

309

Why was I born right here, right now?

— Magna, age 23

310

How many space/time dimensions are in existence in any space and time?

— Donna, age 22

311

Do you cry when we hurt?

— Karen, age 45

312

Many religions today use scare tactics to get people to do what is required. Is that really how you want people to be drawn to you?

— Robin, age 31

313

Is there really a law of Karma?

— Anna, age 47

314

How can I disconnect from emotions that drive me in the wrong directions?

— Garvin, age 39

315

Why doesn't it rain only at night?

— Anna, age 52

316

Could you please speak louder so I can
hear your voice over the others?

— Debbie, age 48

317

Is my little brother all right up there
with you — and is he still that cute
little terror he always was?

— Karly, age 16

318

Do you love each and every human being the same way and not judge them?

— Fatma, age 30

319

Are we living in the last days?

— Jeanette, age 62

320

Why is the voice of intuition so soft?

— Rachelle, age 24

321

Did Darwin get into heaven?

— Alice, age 33

322

Why doesn't every person find his or her true love here on earth?

— Holly, age 44

323

Is it okay to be gay?

— Ron, age 14

324

Are there really aliens and UFOs?

— Evelyn, age 33

325

Is love the answer to every question?

— Francine, age 36

326

The Mets could use another outfielder.
Can you still hit a major league
fastball?

— Ezra, age 30

327

What question would YOU ask YOU if YOU were me?

— Joe, age 35

328

Is Earth a school or classroom?

— Rita, age 59

329

What bothers you the most about us humans?

— Joan, age 53

330

When I die, will I see myself floating away from the world?

— Samuel, age 51

331

How do you determine who our
parents will be?

— Adrial, age 56

332

If someone is a wonderful person, kind
and giving, but does not go to church
or talk about you, can they still get to
heaven?

— Jackie, age 42

333

Is a zebra a black horse with white
stripes or a white horse with black
stripes?

— Tomas, age 34

334

Is there a "rainbow bridge" for our beloved pets?

— Tammy, age 35

335

Why do most people feel the need to hide who they really are?

— Rosa, age 27

336

Why does the "what-if" monster still plague me?

— Rachel, age 27

337

Why did you create religion and caste?
— Rajeev, age 24

338

What is it like to be in your presence?
— Alan, age 50

339

Why are there so many people in
poverty?
— Paul, age 41

340

If you could give me only one
commandment, what would it be?

— Mark, age 49

341

Is there such a thing as time travel?

— Kay, age 41

342

When will you manifest yourself?

— Henry, age 57

343

Why must we believe on "faith" that everything in the Bible is true and correct?

— John, age 56

344

Is anything ever really a "waste" of time?

— Julie, age 31

345

Are you male, female, or beyond gender?

— Rick, age 37

346

How can I be aware of your presence
and your love every minute of every
day?

— Joan, age 59

347

Is believing in you actually believing in
me and my own ability?

— Aleksandar, age 37

If you would like to share the questions YOU
would ask God, or if you have any comments
about this book, please visit our web site:

www.ifyoucouldaskgod.com

About the Authors

Jeff Keller is a motivational speaker and author of the best-selling book, **Attitude is Everything**. For more than 20 years, his presentations, articles, and audio and video programs have inspired people all over the world to develop their full potential. For more information about Jeff, and to sign up for his free monthly e-mail newsletter, Here's To Your Success, go to www.attitudeiseverything.com.

John Lisicich lives in Gig Harbor, Washington, with his awesome wife Sharon. In addition to his work as a sales executive, he devotes considerable time and energy serving his community. In his spare time, John plays the ukulele, loves Hawaiian music, and is fascinated with people and what is in their hearts, minds, and souls around the world.

Printed in the United States
69895LV00008B/64-72